QuickBooks® Desktop Pro 2021

Quick Reference Guide

Comprehensive video training & instruction manuals available at www.teachucomp.com

TEACHUCOMP, INC.®
...it's all about you

The Chart of Accounts

Adding a New Account
1. Select "Lists| Chart of Accounts" from the Menu Bar.
2. Click the "Account" button & choose "New."
3. Choose an account type and click "Continue."
4. Enter the account information and click "Save & Close."

Editing an Account
1. Select "Lists| Chart of Accounts" from the Menu Bar.
2. Click to highlight the account.
3. Click the "Account" button and choose "Edit Account."
4. Edit the information and click "Save & Close."

Deleting or Inactivating an Account
1. Select "Lists| Chart of Accounts" from the Menu Bar.
2. Click to highlight the account.
3. Click the "Account" button and choose "Make Account Inactive" or "Delete Account."
4. Click "OK" to confirm any deleted accounts.

Customers, Employees & Vendors

Accessing the Centers
1. Click "Customers," "Employees" or "Vendors" from the Menu Bar and select the Center from the menu.

Adding a New Customer
1. Click the "Customers & Jobs" tab in the Customer Center.
2. Choose "New Customer" from the "New Customer & Job" drop-down above the tab.
3. Enter all customer information on each of the tabs in the "New Customer" window and click "OK."

Editing or Deleting a Customer
1. Click to highlight the customer in the "Customer & Jobs" tab in the Customer Center.
2. Select "Edit| Edit Customer:Job" *or* "Edit| Delete Customer:Job" from the Menu Bar.
3. If editing, make any changes and then click "OK."

Adding a New Employee
1. Click the "New Employee..." button in the upper-left corner of the Employee Center.
2. Enter all employee information on each of the tabs in the "New Employee" window and click "OK."

Editing or Deleting an Employee
1. Click to highlight the employee on the "Employees" tab in the Employee Center.
2. Select "Edit| Edit Employee" *or* "Edit| Delete Employee from the Menu Bar.
3. If editing, make any changes and then click "OK."

Adding a New Vendor
1. Choose "New Vendor" from the "New Vendor" drop-down in the Vendor Center.
2. Enter all vendor information on each of the tabs in the "New Vendor" window and click "OK."

Editing or Deleting a Vendor
1. Click to highlight the vendor on the "Vendors" tab in the Vendor Center.
2. Select "Edit| Edit Vendor" *or* "Edit| Delete Vendor" from the Menu Bar.
3. If editing, make any changes and then click "OK."

Creating Custom Fields
1. Open the Vendor, Company or Employee Center.
2. Click the "Define Fields" button on the "Additional Info" tab of the "New [list item]" or "Edit [list item]" window. (List item=Vendor, Company or Employee).
3. Enter custom field names and select lists to include.
4. Click "OK."
5. Enter any "Custom Fields" values and click "OK."

Managing List Items

Creating Item List Custom Fields
1. Select "Lists| Item List" from the Menu Bar.
2. Click the "Item" button and then either "New" Or "Edit Item."
3. Click the "Custom Fields" button and then the "Define Fields" button.
4. Enter item label names, select "Use," and click "OK."
5. Enter any "Custom Fields" values and click "OK."
6. For existing custom fields, select "Lists| Item List" from the Menu Bar and select the item. Click the "Item" button and then "Edit Item." Click the "Custom Fields" button, enter values, and click "OK."

Sorting Lists
1. To manually sort, click and drag the diamond next to the item name.
2. To automatically sort, click the column heading.
3. Remove auto sort by clicking the new diamond that appears at the far-left of the column headings.
4. Restore original sort order by selecting "View| Re-Sort List" from the Menu Bar. Then click "OK."

Inactivating and Reactivating Items
1. To inactivate, right-click on an item and choose "Make [list item type] inactive."
2. To show inactive items NOT in a Center list, check the "Include inactive" checkbox.
3. To show inactive items in a Center list, select "All [list item type]" in the "View" menu.
4. To reactivate, show the inactive items within the list and click to remove the "X" next to the item name.

Renaming and Merging List Items
1. To rename, open the "Edit" window of the list item.
2. Type a new name in the name field at the very top of the window.
3. Click the "OK" or "Save and Close" button.
4. To merge, change the name to the same as another item and choose "Yes" when prompted to merge.

Sales Tax

Creating a Sales Tax Item or Group
1. Select "Lists| Item List" from the Menu Bar.
2. Select "New" from the "Item" button pop-up menu.
3. Select "Sales Tax Item" or "Sales Tax Group" from the "Type" drop-down.
4. Enter tax item or group information and click "OK."

Setting Default Sales Tax Preferences
1. Select "Edit| Preferences..." from the Menu Bar.
2. Click "Sales Tax" on the left and then the "Company Preferences" tab on the right.
3. Select preferences and click "OK."

Indicating a Taxable Customer
1. Select "Customers| Customer Center" from the Menu Bar.
2. Click the "Customers & Jobs" tab at the left side.
3. Double-click on the name of the customer in the list.
4. On the "Sales Tax Settings" tab, make selections and click "OK."

Indicating a Taxable Item
1. Select "Lists| Item List" from the Menu Bar.
2. Click to highlight the item.
3. Click the "Item" button and choose "Edit Item."
4. Make the appropriate selection from the "Tax Code" drop-down and click "OK."

Creating a Sales Tax Report
1. Select "Vendors| Sales Tax| Sales Tax Liability" or "Vendors| Sales Tax| Sales Tax Revenue Summary" from the Menu Bar. Change dates, as needed.
2. Click the "X" in the upper-right corner to close.

Paying Sales Tax
1. Select "Vendors| Sales Tax| Pay Sales Tax" from the Menu Bar.
2. Make selections for the account and dates.
3. Click to select the "Pay" column for agencies to pay.
4. Click the "Adjust" button to make any needed tax adjustments and click "OK."
5. Check the "To be printed" checkbox, if desired.
6. Click "OK" to record the payment.

Inventory

Enabling Inventory in QuickBooks
1. Select "Edit|
2. Select "Item
3. Check the "
active" chec
4. Set any pref

Creating I
1. Select "Lists|
2. Select "New" from the "Item" button menu.
3. Select "Inventory Part" from the "Type" drop-down.
4. Enter inventory part information and click "OK."

Creating a Purchase Order
1. Select "Vendors| Create Purchase Orders" from the Menu Bar.
2. Select the vendor from the "Vendor" drop-down.
3. Enter purchase order information and click either the "Save & Close" or "Save & New" button.

Creating Purchase Order Reports
1. Select "Lists| Chart of Accounts" from the Menu Bar.
2. Click to highlight the "Purchase Orders" account.
3. Click the "Reports" button, and select "QuickReport: Purchase Orders" from the menu.

Receiving Inventory with a Bill
1. Select "Vendors| Receive Items and Enter Bill" from the Menu Bar.
2. Select the vendor from the "Vendor" drop-down.
3. Enter bill information and click the "Save & Close" button.

Creating an Item Receipt
1. Select "Vendors| Receive Items" from the Menu Bar.
2. Select the vendor from the "Vendor" drop-down.
3. Enter the receipt information and click the "Save & Close" button.

Matching a Bill to an Item Receipt
1. Select "Vendors| Enter Bill for Received Items" from the Menu Bar.
2. Select the vendor from the "Vendor" drop-down.
3. Select the item receipt and click the "OK" button.
4. Enter the date the bill was received in the "Date" field and click the "Save & Close" button.

Manually Adjusting Inventory
1. Select "Vendors| Inventory Activities| Adjust Quantity/Value on Hand" from the Menu Bar.
2. Select the type of inventory adjustment to make from the "Adjustment Type" drop-down.
3. Make the required adjustments to the inventory.
4. Click the "Save & Close" button.

TeachUcomp, Inc.
Computer Software Training & Continuing Education.
www.teachucomp.com
info@teachucomp.com
877.925.8080

Other Items

Creating Other Items

Create Service Items, Non-Inventory Parts, Other Charges, Subtotals, Groups, Discounts and Payments.

1. Select "Lists| Item list" from the Menu Bar.
2. Select "New" from the "Item" button menu.
3. Select the item type from the "Type" drop-down.
4. Enter the item information and click "OK."

Changing Item Prices

1. Select "Customers| Change Item Prices" from the Menu Bar.
2. Use the "Item Type" drop-down to filter and show only items that match the item type you select.
3. Click the left column to check the item(s) you wish to change.
4. Adjust prices using the fields at the bottom.
5. Click the "Adjust" button and then "OK."

Basic Sales

Creating an Invoice or Sales Receipt

1. Select "Customers| Create Invoices" or "Customers| Enter Sales Receipts" from the Menu Bar.
2. Choose a template from the "Template" drop-down.
3. Use the "Customer:Job" drop-down to select a customer.
4. Enter the invoice or receipt information and click the "Save & Close" or "Save & New" button.

Finding Transactions

1. Open the form window for the type of transaction to find. For example, to find an invoice, open the "Create Invoices" window.
2. Select "Edit| Find [form type]..." from the Menu Bar.
3. Enter the value(s) by which you want to find the transaction and click the "Find" button.
4. Double-click on the item to open it.

Previewing Invoices and Receipts

1. Open the invoice or receipt to preview it.
2. Click the drop-down arrow below the "Print" button in the "Main" tab of the Ribbon.
3. Select the "Preview" command from the drop-down.

Printing Invoices and Receipts

1. Open the sales form to print.
2. Click the "Print" button in the "Main" tab of the Ribbon.
3. Set preferred printing parameters.
4. Click the "Print" button.

Price Levels

Creating New Price Levels

1. Select "Lists| Price Level List" from the Menu Bar.
2. Click the "Price Level" button and select "New" from the pop-up menu.
3. Type the name of the new price level into the "Price Level Name" field.
4. Enter the price level information.
5. Click "OK."

Associating Defaults with a Customer

1. Select "Customer| Customer Center" from the Menu Bar.
2. Double-click on the customer on the "Customers & Jobs" tab of the Customer Center.
3. Select the "Payment Settings" tab in the "Edit Customer" window.
4. Choose the appropriate price level from the "Price Level" drop-down.
5. Click "OK."

Changing Line Item Rates

1. Select the line item in the invoice or receipt.
2. Click into the "Rate" column.
3. Enter the price level.
4. Click "Save & Close."
5. Click "Yes" to confirm, if prompted.

Billing Statements

Setting Finance Charge Preferences

1. Select "Edit| Preferences" from the Menu Bar.
2. Select the Finance Charge icon to the left.
3. Enter desired values on the "Company Preferences" tab and click "OK."

Entering Statement Charges

1. Click to highlight the customer on the "Customers & Jobs" tab of the Customer Center.
2. Select "Customers| Enter Statement Charges" from the Menu Bar.
3. Enter the charge and click the "Record" button.

Creating Statements

1. Select "Customers| Create Statements..." from the Menu Bar.
2. Select statement options, customers and any additional options.
3. Click either the "Preview," "Print," or "E-mail" button to preview or send the statements to the customers.

Payment Processing

Recording a Full Payment

1. Select "Customers| Receive Payments" from the Menu Bar.
2. Select the name of the customer from the "Received From" drop-down.
3. Enter the payment information and click either the "Save & Close" or "Save & New" button.

Entering a Partial Payment

1. Select "Customers| Receive Payments" from the Menu Bar.
2. Select the name of the customer from the "Received From" drop-down.
3. Enter the partial payment information.
4. To attribute the payment to anything other than the oldest invoice, click the "Un-Apply Payment" button on the "Main" tab of the Ribbon.
5. Enter the amount to apply to the appropriate invoice under the "Payment" column.
6. If an underpayment of the total amount due is entered, select the "Write off the extra amount" button to write off the remaining balance, if desired.
7. Click either the "Save & Close" or "Save & New" button.

Applying One Payment to Multiple Invoices

1. Select "Customers| Receive Payments" from the Menu Bar.
2. Select the name of the customer from the "Received From" drop-down.
3. Enter the payment information.
4. To attribute the payment to anything other than the oldest invoice, click the "Un-Apply Payment" button in the "Main" tab of the Ribbon.
5. Enter the amounts that you want to apply to the appropriate invoices in the "Payment" column.
6. Click either the "Save & Close" or "Save & New" button.

Entering Overpayments

1. Select "Customers| Receive Payments" from the Menu Bar.
2. Select the name of the customer from the "Received From" drop-down.
3. Enter the payment information.
4. The overpayment is listed as an "Overpayment" in the bottom left corner. Select either the "Leave the credit to be used later" or the "Refund the amount to the customer" option.
5. Click either the "Save & Close" or "Save & New" button.

Entering Down Payments or Prepayments

1. Select "Customers| Receive Payments" from the Menu Bar.
2. Select the name of the customer from the "Received From" drop-down.
3. Enter the payment information.
4. The down payment or prepayment amount is listed as an "Overpayment" in the bottom left corner. Select the "Leave the credit to be used later" option to apply the credit to the future invoice.
5. Click either "Save & Close" or "Save & New."
6. Click either the "Print Credit Memo" or "OK" button.

Applying Customer Credits

1. Select "Customers| Receive Payments" from the Menu Bar.
2. Select the name of the customer from the "Received From" drop-down.
3. Select the invoice to apply the customer's credit. **Do not** mark it with a checkmark. Instead, select it by clicking on any other column available.
4. Click the "Discounts & Credits" button in the "Main" tab of the Ribbon.
5. On the "Credits" tab, click the checkmark column next to the credit in the "Available Credits" section.
6. To apply a partial credit, change the amount in the "Amt. to Use" column.
7. Click the "Done" button and then either the "Save & Close" or "Save & New" button.

Making Deposits

1. Select "Banking| Make Deposits" from the Menu Bar.
2. In the "Payments to Deposit" window, click to select any payments to deposit and then click "OK."
3. In the "Make Deposits" window, select the bank account from the "Deposit To" drop-down.
4. Enter the date of the deposit into the "Date" field.
5. Click into the next available blank row to record any miscellaneous amounts.
6. Enter any "Cash back" information.
7. Click the drop-down arrow to the right of the toolbar's "Print" button and select either "Deposit Slip" or "Deposit Summary" and then the "Print" button in the "Print" dialog box.
8. Click the "Save & Close" button.

Handling Bounced Checks

1. Select "Customers| Receive Payments..." from the Menu Bar.
2. Locate the payment that contains the bounced check to display it in the "Receive Payments" window by using the "Find" button or the "Previous" and "Next" arrows.
3. Click the "Record Bounced Check" button within the "Main" tab in the Ribbon.
4. Enter the bounced check information and click the "Next" button.
5. Click the "Finish" button to proceed.
6. Click the "Save & Close" button.

Refunding Customer Purchases

Refund a customer's purchase if they return merchandise by creating a credit memo and then issuing a refund check.

1. Select "Customers| Create Credit Memos/Refunds" from the Menu Bar.
2. Select the customer from the "Customer:Job" drop-down.
3. Enter the returned items in the line items area.
4. Click the "Use credit to give refund" button in the "Main" tab of the Ribbon to issue a refund check to the customer.
5. Select the account to withdraw funds for the refund check and any other information needed.
6. Click "OK" and then the "Save & Close" button.
7. Print the refund check and credit memo.

Refunding Customer Payments

Refund a customer's overpayment, down payment or prepayment by issuing a refund check on the credit.

1. Select "Banking| Write Checks" from the Menu Bar.
2. Complete the check information for the refund.
3. Select the "Accounts Receivable" account on the "Expenses" tab.
4. Click the "Save & Close" button & print the check.
5. Select "Customers| Receive Payments" from the Menu Bar and select the customer from the "Received From" drop-down.
6. Click to select the refund check you wrote and then click the "Discounts & Credits" button on the "Main" tab in the ribbon.
7. Choose the credit that matched the refund check amount on the "Credits" tab.
8. Click the "Done" and "Save and Close" buttons.

Entering and Paying Bills

Entering a Bill

1. Select "Vendors| Enter Bills" from the Menu Bar.
2. Choose a vendor from the "Vendor" drop-down.
3. Enter all bill information and click the "Save & Close" or "Save & New" button.

Paying a Bill

1. Select "Vendors| Pay Bills" from the Menu Bar.
2. Click the checkbox to the left of the bill(s) to pay.
3. Change the "Amt. to Pay" column for any partial payments.
4. Complete the bill payment information and click the "Pay Selected Bills" button.

Applying Early Payment Discounts

1. Select "Vendors| Pay Bills" from the Menu Bar.
2. Click the checkbox to the left of the bill to pay.
3. Click the "Set Discount" button.
4. Enter the discount amount, the account used to track payment discounts, and then click "Done."
5. In the "Pay Bills" window, complete the bill payment information and then click the "Pay Selected Bills" button.

Entering a Vendor Credit

1. Select "Vendors| Enter Bills" from the Menu Bar.
2. Select the "Credit" option at the top of the form.
3. Complete the credit information and any affected accounts or items on the "Expenses" and "Items" tabs and click the "Save & Close" button.

Applying a Vendor Credit

1. Select "Vendors| Pay Bills" from the Menu Bar.
2. Click the checkbox to the left of the bill to pay.
3. Click the "Set Credits" button.
4. To use only a portion of the credit, type the amount to apply within the "Amt. To Use" column.
5. Click the "Done" button.
6. In the "Pay Bills" window, complete the bill payment information and click the "Pay Selected Bills" button.

Bank Accounts

Entering Transactions in the Register

1. Close any open screens within QuickBooks and then select "Banking| Use Register" from the Menu Bar.
2. Select the account from the drop-down and click "OK."
3. Record entry in the next available blank row and click the "Record" button.

Using the "Write Checks" Window

1. Select "Banking| Write Checks" from the Menu Bar.
2. Select the appropriate checking account from the "Bank Account" drop-down.
3. Enter all check information.
4. On the "Expenses" tab, enter the accounts and amounts to attribute to the check.
5. Click the "Save & Close" or "Save & New" button.

Writing a Check for Inventory Items

1. Select "Banking| Write Checks" from the Menu Bar.
2. Enter all the check information.
3. On the "Items" tab, select the inventory part from the "Item" drop-down and enter a quantity.
4. Click either the "Save & Close" or "Save & New" button.

Printing a Single Check

1. Select "Banking| Write Checks" from the Menu Bar.
2. Use the "Previous" and "Next" arrows or the "Find" button to display the check.
3. Click the drop-down arrow on the "Print" button in the "Main" tab of the Ribbon.
4. Choose "Check" from the drop-down and then "OK."
5. Set any desired printing options in the "Print Checks" dialog box and click the "Print" button.

Printing a Batch of Checks

1. Select "Banking| Write Checks" from the Menu Bar.
2. Click the drop-down arrow on the "Print" button in the "Main" tab of the Ribbon and select "Batch."
3. Click to un-check (de-select) any checks ***not*** to print.
4. Select a bank account, enter a first check number and click "OK."
5. Set any desired printing options in the "Print Checks" dialog box and click the "Print" button.

Transferring Funds

1. Select "Banking| Transfer Funds" from the Menu Bar.
2. Enter the transfer information.
3. Click either "Save & Close" or "Save & New."

Voiding Checks

1. Select "Banking| Write Checks" from the Menu Bar.
2. Use the "Previous" and "Next" arrows or the "Find" button to display the check.
3. Select "Edit| Void [type] Check" from the Menu Bar.
4. Click "Save & Close," then "Yes" to confirm changes.

Reporting

Creating a QuickReport

1. Select an item in a list, open a transaction form, or otherwise display the data.
2. Press "Ctrl + Q" on your keyboard.
3. To close the report, press the "Escape" key.

QuickZooming a Report

1. Place the mouse pointer on data in the report or graph until a magnifying glass with a "Z" appears and double-click.
2. The original transaction information or another report showing the transaction appears.
3. To close the report, press the "Escape" key.

Modifying a Report

1. **To modify a report based on a preset report,** open the desired preset report to use as the basis for the custom report and click the "Customize Report" button in the toolbar. ***Or,* to create a new transaction detail or summary report from scratch,** select "Reports| Custom Reports" from the Menu Bar and then choose "Transaction Detail" or "Summary" from the menu.
2. In the "Modify Report" dialog box, make the desired changes on the "Display," "Filters," "Header/Footer," and "Fonts & Numbers" tabs.
3. Click "OK" to modify the report settings.

Customizing Report Columns

1. **To rearrange report columns,** place the mouse over the name of a column in the heading until the pointer turns into a "hand" icon. Click, drag, and release in the desired location.
2. **To resize columns in a report,** place the mouse pointer to the right of the name of the column to resize, where the three vertical dots are located, until the mouse pointer changes into a thin vertical line intersected by a horizontal arrow. Click, drag left or right, and release to resize.

Memorizing Modified Reports

1. Click the "Memorize" button in the toolbar at the top of the modified report's window.
2. Enter a report name in the "Name" field.
3. Check and select a "Memorized Report Group," if desired and then click "OK."

Printing Reports

1. Click the "Print" button in the toolbar of the report and select "Report" from the drop-down.
2. Set print options in the "Print Reports" window.
3. Set options and click the "Print" button.

Batch Printing Forms

1. Select "File| Print Forms" from the Menu Bar.
2. Select the type of form to print from the side menu, select the forms, set printing options, and click "OK."

Estimating

Creating a New Job

1. Select "Customers| Customer Center" from the Menu Bar.
2. Select the customer in the "Customers & Jobs" list.
3. Click the "New Customer & Job" button and choose the "Add Job" command.
4. Enter a name for the job into the "Job Name" field.
5. Enter the job information on the "Job Info" tab.
6. Click "OK."

Creating an Estimate

1. Select "Customers| Create Estimates" from the Menu Bar.
2. Select the job from the "Customer:Job" drop-down.
3. Complete the estimate information.
4. Click either "Save & Close" or "Save & New."

Invoicing from an Estimate

1. Select "Customers| Create Invoices" from the Menu Bar.
2. Select the job from the "Customer:Job" drop-down.
3. In the "Available Estimates" window, select the estimate from which to create the invoice.
4. Click "OK."
5. In the "Create Progress Invoice Based on Estimate" window, select an invoicing option and click "OK."
6. Verify the invoice information and either click the "Save & Close" or "Save & New" button.

Inactivating an Estimate

1. Select "Customers| Create Estimates" from the Menu Bar.
2. Use the "Previous" and "Next" arrows or the "Find" button to display the estimate.
3. Click the "Mark As Inactive" button on the "Main" tab. Click "Save & Close" and then "Yes."

Making Purchases for a Job

1. Open the purchasing form, such as the "Create Purchase Orders," "Enter Bills," "Write Checks," or "Enter Credit Card Charges" window.
2. Enter the vendor information.
3. Enter the first "Item" or record the expense for the job in the line items area.
4. For each line item entered, use the drop-down to select the "Customer:Job" to be billed.
5. Click the "Save & Close" or "Save & New" button.

Invoicing for Job Costs

1. Select "Customers| Create Invoices" from the Menu Bar.
2. Select the job from the "Customer:Job" drop-down.
3. In the "Billable Time/Costs" window, click the "Select the outstanding billable time and costs to add to this invoice?" option button and then click "OK."
4. Click the left column to select expenses to bill.
5. Enter all billable items and expenses and click "OK."
6. Complete the invoice and select "Save & New" or "Save and Close."

Creating Jobs Reports

1. Select "Reports| Jobs, Time & Mileage" from the Menu Bar and click the report name in the menu.

Time Tracking

Printing Blank Weekly Timesheets

1. Select "Employees| Enter Time| Use Weekly Timesheet" from the Menu Bar.
2. Click the drop-down arrow to the right of the "Print" button and select "Print Blank Timesheet."
3. Click the "Print" button.

Using a Weekly Timesheet

1. Select "Employees| Enter Time| Use Weekly Timesheet" from the Menu Bar.
2. Choose a name and date at the top of the window.
3. Enter the timesheet information in the columns.
4. Click either "Save & Close" or "Save & New."

Using the "Time/Enter Single Activity" Window

1. Select "Employees| Enter Time| Time / Enter Single Activity" from the Menu Bar.
2. Enter the employee activity information and click either "Save & Close" or "Save & New."

Invoicing a Customer Based on Time

1. Select "Customers| Create Invoices" from the Menu Bar.
2. Use the "Customer:Job" drop-down to select the customer:job to which you have assigned billable time.
3. In the "Billable Time/Costs" window, click the "Select the outstanding billable time and costs to add to this invoice?" option and then "OK."
4. In the "Choose Billable Time and Costs" window, click the "Time" tab, and select hours to bill the customer by clicking the line item's leftmost column.
5. Click "OK" and then "Save & Close" or "Save & New."

Displaying Time Tracking Reports

1. Select "Reports| Jobs, Time & Mileage" from the Menu Bar.
2. Click to select the report name in the menu.

Entering Vehicle Mileage

1. Select "Company| Enter Vehicle Mileage..." from the Menu Bar.
2. Enter all vehicle, job and mileage information.
3. To enter mileage rates, click the "Mileage Rates" button at the top of the window, enter the rate information and click the "Close" button.
4. Click "Save & Close" or "Save & New."

Invoicing a Customer for Mileage

1. Select "Customers| Create Invoices" from the Menu Bar.
2. Use the "Customer:Job" drop-down to select the customer:job to which you have assigned billable mileage.
3. In the "Billable Time/Costs" window, click the "Select the outstanding billable time and costs to add to this invoice?" option and then "OK."
4. Click the "Mileage" tab in the "Choose Billable Time/Costs" window, then select the mileage to bill by clicking the line item's leftmost column.
5. Click "OK."
6. Click "Save & Close" or "Save & New."

Payroll

Viewing and Creating Payroll Items

1. **To view the current set of payroll items,** select "Lists| Payroll Item List" from the Menu Bar.
2. **To add a new payroll item,** click the "Payroll Item" button in the lower-left corner of the "Payroll Item List" and then select "New."
3. In the "Add new payroll item" window, answer the questions and click the "Next" button on each screen until the new item is set up.
4. Click "Finish."

Setting Employee Payroll Defaults

1. Select "Employees| Employee Center" from the Menu Bar.
2. Click the "Manage Employee Information" button in the toolbar and select the "Change New Employee Default Settings" command.
3. Enter default information and click "OK."

Setting Up Employee Payroll Information

1. Select "Employees| Employee Center" from the Menu Bar.
2. Click the "New Employee" button to open the "New Employee" window, or double-click an existing employee on the "Employees" tab to open the "Edit Employee" window.
3. Click the "Payroll Info" tab and enter all the employee's payroll information and then click "OK."

Creating or Editing a Payroll Schedule

1. Select "Employees| Add or Edit Payroll Schedules" from the Menu Bar.
2. **To create a new schedule,** click the "Payroll Schedule" button and then choose "New." Enter the schedule information and click "OK."
3. **To edit an existing schedule,** click to select the schedule in the "Payroll Schedule List" window. Click the "Payroll Schedule" button, and then choose "Edit Payroll Schedule." Enter the schedule information and click "OK."

Creating Scheduled Paychecks

1. Select "Employees| Pay Employees| Scheduled Payroll" from the Menu Bar.
2. On the "Pay Employees" tab, select the name of the payroll schedule and click the "Start Scheduled Payroll" button.
3. To make changes to a paycheck, click the hyperlinked employee name in the list to open the paycheck in the "Preview Paycheck" window. Edit the information and click "Save & Close."
4. Click the "Continue" button.
5. Review the summary and select "Check Options."
6. Click the "Create Paychecks" button.
7. Click the "Print Paychecks" and "Print Pay Stubs" buttons, as needed.
8. Click the "Close" button.

Creating Unscheduled Paychecks

1. Select "Employees| Pay Employees| Unscheduled Payroll" from the Menu Bar.
2. Enter the payroll information, and click to place a checkmark next to the names of employees to pay.
3. Click the "Continue" button.
4. Review the Summary and select "Check Options."
5. Click on the hyperlinked name of any employee shown within the list to edit the payroll information if needed, and click "Save & Close."
6. Click the "Create Paychecks" button.
7. Click the "Print Paychecks" and "Print Pay Stubs" buttons as needed, and then click "Close."

Creating Termination Paychecks

1. Select "Employees| Pay Employees| Termination Check" from the Menu Bar.
2. Enter the payroll information, and click to place a checkmark next to the names of employees to pay.
3. In the "Release Date" column, enter the employee's release date and then click the "Continue" button.
4. Click either the "Make Inactive" or "Keep as Active" button to continue.
5. Review the Summary and select "Check Options."
6. Click on the hyperlinked name of any employee shown within the list to edit the payroll information if needed, and click "Save & Close."
7. Click the "Create Paychecks" button.
8. Click the "Print Paychecks" and "Print Pay Stubs" buttons as needed, and then click "Close."

Credit Card Accounts

Creating a Credit Card Account

1. Select "Lists| Chart of Accounts" from the Menu Bar.
2. Click the "Account" button & select "New."
3. Select the "Credit Card" option and click "Continue."
4. Enter the account information and click "Save & Close" or "Save & New."

Entering Credit Card Charges

1. Select "Banking| Enter Credit Card Charges" from the Menu Bar.
2. Select the card from the "Credit Card" drop-down.
3. Enter all credit card charge information and click "Save & Close" or "Save & New."

Reconciling a Credit Card Account

1. Select "Banking| Reconcile" from the Menu Bar.
2. Select the account from the "Account" drop-down.
3. Enter the statement date, ending balance, and any finance charges, then click the "Continue" button.
4. Click the checkmark column to mark any cleared transactions.
5. Click the "Reconcile Now" button.
6. Select an option to either write a check or enter a bill to pay the credit card bill and click "OK."
7. Select an option in the "Select Reconciliation Report" dialog box. Click "Display," "Print," or "Close."
8. Select the company to pay in the "Write Checks" or "Enter Bills" window and click "Save & Close."

The Loan Manager

Using the Loan Manager

To add a loan to the Loan Manager:

1. Select "Banking| Loan Manager" from the Menu Bar.
2. Click the "Add a Loan" button.
3. Enter the loan information on each screen and click "Next" until the wizard is complete.
4. Click the "Finish" button.

To edit or delete a loan in the Loan Manager:

1. Select "Banking| Loan Manager" from the Menu Bar and click the loan name in the "Loan List" section.
2. Click the "Edit Loan Details" button to return to the wizard to edit the loan, or click the "Remove Loan" button and "Yes" to remove.

Company Management

Updating Company Information

1. Select "Company| My Company" from the Menu Bar.
2. Click the "Edit" button.
3. Edit the company information and click "OK."

Using Reminders & Setting Preferences

1. Select "Edit| Preferences..." from the Menu Bar.
2. Click "Reminders" from the scroll box at the left.
3. Click the "My Preferences" tab, and select "Show Reminders List when opening a Company file."
4. Click "OK."

Making General Journal Entries

1. Select "Company| Make General Journal Entries..." from the Menu Bar.
2. Click to select the accounts involved in the transaction and enter the credit and debit amounts.
3. Click "Save & Close" to post the transaction.

ISBN 978-1-941854-68-6

9 781941 854686

Made in the USA